T0128983

Aging With Grace and Purpose

Words To Inspire Us
In Advancing Years

Practical Suggestions
For Planning Ahead

Lois Berry

iUniverse, Inc.
Bloomington

Aging with Grace and Purpose

iUniverse books may be ordered through booksellers or by contacting:

iUniverse
1663 Liberty Drive
Bloomington, IN 47403
www.iuniverse.com
1-800-Authors (1-800-288-4677)

Because of the dynamic nature of the Internet, any web addresses or links
contained in this book may have changed since publication and may no longer be
valid. The views expressed in this work are solely those of the author and do not
necessarily reflect the views of the publisher, and the publisher hereby disclaims
any responsibility for them.

Any people depicted in stock imagery provided by Thinkstock are models,
and such images are being used for illustrative purposes only.

Certain stock imagery © Thinkstock.

ISBN: 978-1-4620-6995-8 (sc)
ISBN: 978-1-4620-6996-5 (e)

Printed in the United States of America

iUniverse rev. date: 12/13/2011

Table of Contents

ACKNOWLEDGMENTS

To all the people who helped me grow in my life's journey. That would certainly include my family who had the most profound effect on me. The events of my early life helped shape me into the person I became. Later there was my husband, Ben, and children Jody, Jim, Ruthie and Barbara. Later there are six grandchildren – Kelly, Jaime, Ronee, Mark, Jeff and Jenn and their spouses Chris, Matt, Mark, Casey and Ginnie. So far they have added six great grandchildren: Meredith, Tommy, Rylee, Reagan, Berkeley and Luke. I am pretty amazed to have begun all that. They are all responsible, productive and loving and have taught me many things. Also, there are too many friends and acquaintances who have enriched my life to name but they will know who they are.

My special gratitude to daughter, Jody Meredith, and daughter-in-law, Chris Berry. Each of them read this book and made helpful corrections and suggestions. My son, Jim, kept my computer functioning and helped me put the final manuscript together.

INTRODUCTION

Why would I presume to give advice to anyone? I am not a psychologist, a psychiatrist, nor do I have a degree in counseling. What I do have is a degree in living. I often wish I had the wisdom when I was younger that I seem to have acquired in old age. I have lived through traumatic events in my childhood without outside help to assist me in recovery.

Growing up during the depression, I still managed to go to college, get married and have four children. During the fifties, my husband and I both had life-threatening illnesses and survived. The children grew up, left home and moved on with their own lives. Life was different again. If I've learned anything, it's to be flexible and go with the flow.

Another big adjustment came when my husband died at the age of 71 and I had to learn to live alone. I had never lived alone in my life so that was a completely new experience. Eventually, this period of my life gave me the time to write two books. One, titled Cancer Saved My Life, told my story of surviving breast cancer that metastasized to the bone and how it changed my life. The other, The Doctor Who Dared To Be Different, is about my remarkable oncologist.

In spite of, or because of some difficult times, there still were times of happiness and great joy. Actually, when I review my long life, I tend to remember the good times more than the bad. I've learned so much and I would like to share some of it with you.

WHAT HAPPENED?
HOW DID I GET OLD?

Old age creeps up on a person. I know that is hard to believe, but I can testify to the fact that I don't know how I arrived at 90 plus years of age. When you are 40 or 50 life seems as if it will go on forever. Then the years seem to suddenly accelerate and there you are – an old person. Because I have been granted such a long life, I have learned a few things about living. It hasn't been easy and I've made many mistakes, but, hopefully, I'm a better person because of the process. I decided a long time ago that it's alright to make mistakes if you learn from them.

No one likes to think about getting old and dependent on others. That is precisely why we need to think ahead and make some plans. Of course we don't know what the future will bring. So we need to make plans that fit different possibilities.

Most any plan will assume that we are in reasonably good health. If that is not the case, then it is a whole different situation.

I have learned that the accumulation of money and possessions does not bring happiness in the long run. It is good to have a rewarding job and adequate funds to live comfortably. After that, what becomes most important is loving and giving back to those less fortunate.

The kind of loving I mean is an all-encompassing, unconditional love. Over the years, I have had to work very hard not to be judgmental. I think we have all had the experience of meeting someone and without ever knowing that person we decide we don't like them. I finally learned to reserve my judgment. We have no idea of that person's past or the challenges they have had to meet. If we take the time to know them, we may find that they are a person of great depth and courage.

There are rewards, of course, in living a long time, but old age is often difficult because of physical and/or mental problems. As we get older we lose a lot of mobility, but I try to be grateful for what I have left.

I'm sure you notice, as I do, that many old people get difficult and complaining. These people are not much fun to be around so I try hard to be as pleasant as possible. Most of us do lose the energy we used to have and are not as strong physically. However, if we can take care of ourselves with some help and still have our mind, we should thank God everyday. At the end of each day think of the good things that have happened – often unexpected.

We should try hard not to be set in our ways and cooperate with those who are trying to assist us in making decisions. I like the word "flexible" in my relationships with others. We try to hang onto life as we've known it for many years. However, it is entirely possible that physically and/or financially we cannot continue to live the way we want. We should be grateful and loving if we do have those willing to assist us. If you do not have anyone to assist you in making decisions, there are agencies in your community to help you and I will list those possibilities later. But do believe me, if you live a long time you cannot continue to live without help.

As we age, we need to be realistic and make plans for the future. Of course we don't know how much of a future we have, but we need to make plans for what may lay ahead for us. If the time comes when you need to move, you should be close to family if possible.

In my own case, I have been a widow for many years and managed for years to stay in my home. It was a lovely place with a beautiful view and I enjoyed being there. I thought I would remain there as long as I lived.

I had recovered from numerous health problems. I was 85 years old when a voice said to me, "Time to move on." I sold the house and moved to an apartment building that had recently been constructed nearby. It was important for me to stay in the same area where I have spent many years. So this was a good solution for me although it is not always possible for everyone. I did consider buying a condominium, but decided it was not a good investment at my age.

Your decisions are going to be very different if you are a couple than if you are alone. If you live alone and need to have surgery or spend time in a hospital, you will have to hire help at home or go to a nursing home for rehabilitation. Sometimes it is possible to stay with family while you recover, but I wouldn't count on that.

In planning ahead, so much depends on the state of our health. It is hard to admit that we are aging and less able to take care of ourselves.

SO------WHERE DO WE START?

IS YOUR LIFE WORTH LIVING?

When we reach old age and, hopefully, are still in reasonably good health, it is the time when we can think about our past and what the future may hold. Since we are here, we might as well make the most of the time we have left. We can be positive and fun to be with. Or we can be negative and constantly complaining. We can always find fault with something since we don't live in a perfect world. Years ago I was blessed to have a friend who was always cheerful. I knew she had suffered tragedies in her life so I said to her one day, "You are always so much fun to be with and you never talk about the heartaches in your life." She replied, "I learned long ago that people want to hear about your troubles for about two weeks. After that, they tend to avoid you." I think of her remarks often and try to be positive no matter what is going on in my life.

Of course, having a positive outlook on life doesn't suddenly happen. We need to work on our attitude about life and our relationship with others long before old age. If we have not been pleasant to be with during our lifetime, it is not going to happen suddenly in old age.

It is not always automatic or easy to stay positive as we age. My husband died of heart failure at the age of 71 and I have been alone now for twenty-one years. I had never lived alone as I lived at home until I was married. When I began a life alone, I realized that I had always thought of myself as half of something after marriage. When I lost my husband I thought I would fall apart. But I did not. I realized that I could be alone. This was a different attitude for me. I guess you find things in yourself that you never knew existed.

I have found that reaching out to others lifts my spirits and I feel better. We need to find a cause that we feel passionate about and give of our time and/ or money. As we age, we don't have the same energy and may not be physically able to be actively involved. But we can make phone calls, send emails, write and contribute financially.

Learning to be a good listener is a great skill. Unless friends ask specifically for advice, what they really want is someone to listen to them. Can you learn to be a good listener? If you have a hobby, you can develop that skill. I like to write and have had time to do more of that. It is rewarding to me and, I hope, helpful to others.

I, personally, don't know how a person can be positive without some kind of faith. So many people spend a lifetime searching for religion. I have a friend who says he has been searching for faith all his life but has really never found it. Then he goes on to say that he is a better person because of his search.

Faith is such a personal thing. Some people say they have all the answers and I think that is wonderful. I believe that what is most important is that I never feel alone. I feel surrounded by a wonderful presence that sustains me, loves me and cares for me. There are so many different faiths and religions each thinking they have all the answers. I would never presume to tell people what to believe, but I would hope that they do believe in another power beside themselves. In my circumstances, I can't imagine not having a faith that sustains me. Feeling that I am not alone in this life journey has helped to sustain me when times are difficult. I will go into detail about my search for faith in the Chapter titled Spiritual Journey.

I feel fortunate that I have a positive attitude about life. I do feel that if today is sad or difficult tomorrow will be better. I do feel that life is worth living because I am curious about what happens next. As I age, I would like to be pleasant to be around.

I would like to share the following with you that speaks to me in a profound way. I do not know the author but my notes say it is from the Spiritual Letters Section of Library Online, Inc.

"Dear Lord:

You know better than I know myself that I am getting older and will some day be old. Keep me from the fatal habit of thinking that I must say something on every subject and on every occasion. Release me from craving to straighten out everybody's affairs. Make me thoughtful but not moody, helpful but not bossy. With my vast store of wisdom, it seems a pity not to use it all, but you know, Lord, that I want a few friends at the end.

"Keep my mind free from the recital of endless details, give me the wings to get to the point. Seal my lips on my aches and pains – they are increasing. And the love of rehearsing them is becoming sweeter as the years go by. I dare not ask for grace enough to enjoy the tales of other's pains, but help me to endure them with patience. I dare not ask for improved memory but for a growing humility and a lessening cocksureness when my memory seems to clash with the memories of others. Teach me the glorious lesson that occasionally

I may be mistaken. Keep me reasonably sweet. I do not want to be a saint – some of them are so hard to live with – but a sour old person is one of the crowning works of evil. Give me the ability to see good things in unexpected people, and give me, O Lord, the grace to tell them so. Amen"

DON'T JUST SIT THERE DO SOMETHING

Even though a move is not imminent, there are positive steps we can take to make any later transition easier. It is an overwhelming task to most of us. We have managed to collect an enormous amount of "stuff" in our lifetime. It is so easy to make excuses for not addressing the problem. I found that instead of looking at the total project and the enormity of accomplishing it, it was better for me to take one small area at a time.

For instance, I would take an area of the kitchen. Empty out a section of drawers, sort out what I wanted to keep and put the rest in boxes to be given away or be thrown away. Clean out the drawer and put back what you want to keep. If you do this a small area at a time, when it comes time to move everything left goes to your new place.

I love books and I had a large collection. I kept most of the ones on medical issues and gave most of my books on religion to my church. Those that were left after I had sorted and decided which ones to keep were sold to a second hand bookstore. Since then, I have found out that if I had given them to my local library, I could have taken a tax deduction.

Personal cards and letters from children, grandchildren and friends are difficult to part with. I had been saving them for years and there were sacks and sacks of them in my downstairs storage. As much as I hated to part with them, I decided that neither I nor anyone else would ever read them again. So, reluctantly, they went to the recycle bin. Many people save magazines and/or papers that they plan to read at a later time. Eventually, they pile up everywhere. Now is the time to be honest with yourself. Are you ever going to read any of that accumulation? If not, get rid of it.

Depending on your age, health and living situation, you might also want to give away things like your good china, silverware and crystal. After many years of cooking and entertaining, I really didn't want to do that anymore. It makes you feel good to pass on your nice things to children or grandchildren.

There are professional services that you can hire to help you downsize and move. I have friends who have done that and have been well satisfied with this assistance. I was fortunate that I had children who helped with sorting and disposing of things.

If you have a sizable amount of furniture and other household items, there are several ways to dispose of them. You can have a garage sale. That takes time and effort to arrange and price your leftover belongings. There are businesses that will do this for you and take a commission on the sales. Another option is to give to a charitable organization and take a tax deduction. In my area there is an organization called Share House. They are a good option because they will pick up what you want to donate. They will take anything including furniture, linens, dishes and pots and pans. They have a warehouse where eligible people can come and pick up what they need. I like this organization because there is no charge to the recipient. If you are donating to a charity, be sure to ask if they will pick up all the items that you want to donate and not just selective items.

Now ---we will assume you have downsized your entire house. What a good feeling to be living in a clutter free atmosphere.

I am going to list other things that you need to have in order and on file.

It is absolutely essential that you put your affairs in order. You need to have a Will, a physicians directive and power of attorney to a trusted family member or if that is not possible, perhaps a lawyer. If you are going to have a lawyer help you, ask him/her how much they charge for the services you need. You can shop for a lawyer who will charge what you can afford. Certainly you need to have an outside person help with your Will. Unless your estate is very complicated this is relatively easy. At the time you prepare your Will, you should name an executor. The executor executes your desires after your death. The physicians directive is fairly straightforward and your doctor and member of your family should have a copy. This document just instructs anyone in the medical profession not to use extraordinary measures to keep you alive in the event of a terminal illness. The power of attorney is given in case you cannot take care of yourself. Otherwise, it is never used in your lifetime. I believe that individuals neglect to take care of all of the above because they are often in a state of denial. About what, you say? They don't want to think about the fact that they may die someday. Well, let me assure you that it's going to happen and it will be so much easier for your loved ones if they know what you desire. So---don't put your head in the sand. We don't need to be morbid but we need to be realistic.

Next we need to analyze our finances for now and in the future. So much depends on how long we live.

This is discussed in the chapter that evaluates how much money we have now and for the future.

WILL MY MONEY LAST
MY LIFETIME?

You will probably say that is a silly question since you have no idea how long you are going to live. True enough but, realistically, people are living well into their 80s. Taking into account that there are accidents or terminal illnesses, I believe it is better to be prepared. How much better to have too much money than not enough.

To accomplish this goal takes long term planning, First of all, let me say---- SAVE SAVE SAVE. Start at an early age to put some money into a savings account every month. The first check you write each month should be to yourself. It doesn't have to be much but usually if you wait until the end of the month there is nothing left. When you have accumulated enough money in your savings account, invest it. This necessitates selecting a financial advisor to help you in making decisions. I made mistakes at first, but the advisor I have had for over twenty-five years has been a great blessing. Be careful not to pick someone who wants to buy and sell often. This is called "churning" your account and that person will end up making more then you do. My advice is to buy good solid investments with the help of a financial planner and hold as you build an estate.

The ideal situation will be if you don't have to use your capital but can live off the income from your investments plus other income. Unless you save and plan ahead the money isn't going to suddenly be there when you retire. As I write this, our country is going through economic woes and a recession. I believe a person should not panic, but hope that a recovery is forthcoming.

Of course any planning assumes that you are reasonably well. It is not possible to plan for all contingencies such as health problems and/or the inability to take care of yourself.

My thinking is influenced by the fact that I grew up during the great depression. My family was very poor and I was determined not to be poor when I was old. In those days, we didn't have credit cards and we couldn't buy anything until we had the money to pay for it. What a concept! In fact, I think that enormous credit card debt is part of our present economic problems. In my opinion, it is individuals purchasing things without any concrete idea of how they are going to pay for it. It's been called "instant gratification".

I remember times when I was growing up when I wanted something desperately. By the time I had enough money to buy it, I often didn't want it anymore. That taught me a lesson for the rest of my life. I don't buy things impulsively. I make sure I really want or need something and can afford it before I spend any money.

Making plans for the future depends largely on finances so we need to analyze what our financial situation is now and how we plan for the future. I think that it is important that we do not live beyond our means. Make a budget considering your income and expenses and try to stick to it. There are always unexpected expenses but you can manage those if you are not running up large credit bills. You can save toward that cruise or trip to Hawaii or wherever, but it is foolish to max out your credit cards without knowing how you're going to pay them off. I see many good people in denial about their declining health and/or their ability to maintain their housing or the resources to pay for help.

So – let's start by making a list of our income and expenses. This will include discretionary income that you can save or spend.

MONTHLY INCOME:

From employment if still working or retirement
benefits such as 401K , IRA or annuity

Social Security when that becomes applicable.

Dividends and Interest from investments

Sale of Home if and when that becomes a reality.

Profit from sale of home invested for income.

PRESENT EXPENSES

Mortgage payments

Property Taxes

Yard Maintenance

Security System

Heating

Garbage Collection

Sewer and Water

Property Maintenance

Insurance which would include:

Car

Homeowners

Umbrella Policy

Health:Medicare, Supplemental, Long

Term Care

In this list I have included mostly just fixed
expenses. It does not include such discretionary
spending as food, entertainment, clothes, vacations
and the like.

Now that you have a realistic idea of your finances, the next question is where can I afford to live if I decided that I need to move? If your home is too large or expensive to maintain, you could sell your home and use the proceeds from that sale to buy a condo. I have friends who have done that and are happy with that decision. You will still have many of the same expenses. In addition to a possible mortgage, there will be property taxes and maintenance. You can determine ahead what those expenses will be and buy what you can afford. If you are thinking of buying an older condo, be sure to inquire if there are any major maintenance projects that will require assessments to condo owners. Such as, new roofs and outside painting of buildings or any major landscaping.

Retirement Homes: This seems to be a solution for many retirees. There are different options and you need to ask questions before making a decision. First, you want to locate places in the area where you want to live. Every community has free services that will identify retirement homes and what they have to offer. Look on the internet on your computer or in the phone book. Of course you will want to inspect the property, but you also need to ask the following questions:

Is there a fee for buying into the facility? If so, how much and what will be refunded if you move or die? This is usually a large amount and not all retirement homes require it. Others keep a portion and refund the remainder to the buyer or their heirs.

What is the monthly fee and what does it cover? It usually covers cleaning and dinner. Does the size of your apartment depend on what you pay?

Ask if they have social activities for residents if that is important to you.

Be sure to ask if the retirement home has skilled nursing care. If you move later in life, you need to be sure you won't have to move again. I had a close friend who thought she was taking care of herself for the rest of her life. She was a widow and had no children and she thought she had made a good decision when she moved into a beautiful retirement home. She had a nice small apartment, there was a swimming pool and a lovely dining room. She was very content until she got sick and then they told her to move. They had no skilled nursing care. The remainder of this lady's life was a hectic series of moves trying to find a place she could stay until she died. Some places have what they call "assisted living". This consists of things like bringing meals to your apartment, assistance with medication, etc. There is a charge for any of these extras and they do not include total care. So there you are – back at square one with no place to stay.

I think any of us would like to stay in our own place if possible physically and financially. Maybe you can manage that with part time help. If you have to have full time help around the clock, it is enormously expensive and is not covered by Medicare or other insurance. I made the decision when I was in my mid eighties to sell my home and now live in a very nice apartment where I don't have to worry about all those maintenance problems associated with home ownership. My health is reasonably good and I have help for cleaning and grocery shopping a few hours each week. Otherwise, I take care of myself. So far so good.

If you need to move to a nursing home because of your inability to take care of yourself, you are responsible for the costs until you have used up all of your money. So it is very important before you make this move to ask the nursing home you have chosen if they accept Medicaid when and if you run out of money,

Believe it or not, we have a lady in our church who is 105 and was evicted from the nursing home where she lived when she ran out of money because they don't accept Medicaid patients. That is so outrageous but shows that you need to be sure the nursing home won't abandon you when your funds are exhausted. My friend said, "I should have asked but I certainly didn't think I would live to 105. Her body has failed her, but her mind is still very sharp.

If your physical or mental needs require that you move into a nursing home and you are interested in a particular place, you can contact them directly to find out about costs and services. Many people do not know that Medicare does not usually pay for nursing care. If a patient is sent to a nursing home directly from a hospital, Medicare will pay for care for a short period. If you enter a nursing home directly from your residence, the patient is responsible for the costs until any money they have is used up. Then they are eligible for Medicaid. That is why it is so important to know if the nursing home you move into accepts Medicaid patients.

Still another option is an Adult Family Home. They have more of a home atmosphere instead of an institutional setting and take fewer residents. If you have a computer, you will find information about location and the kind of care they offer. If you find that an adult home might fill your needs, the following is a good list of questions to ask that were published in the Seattle Time.

Check the enforcement history which can be found at the Department of Social and Health services website.

Does the owner live in the home? Who provides care? It is important to meet the actual caregivers and ask about their training and qualifications.

What are the scheduled activities? Access to daily activities is important to active seniors. Does the home provide transportation to stores and activities?

Does it schedule activities such as exercise classes and games?

What are the staffing levels? Staffing is a critical measure of good care. Determine whether the home has 24 hour staffing. If not, how does a disabled or bedridden resident get to the bathroom at night? How does a resident summon help at night?

Make unscheduled tours to observe staffing and general well being of residents.

Ask for references.

Perhaps you will always be able to live in your home. Usually, it depends on how long you live and if you can afford to have more help to keep your chosen lifestyle going. You are fortunate if you are a couple. Of course there are the obvious benefits of companionship and having another person to share in everyday living. Then, I believe it is possible to live in your home longer because you can help each other if you have health problems.

One thing I might add to this discourse is to be sure to wear a Lifeline if you live alone. It is important to be able to call for help if you fall or feel ill.

ESTABLISH GOOD RELATIONSHIPS

We don't live in a vacuum. There are all those other people in the world – parents, siblings, teachers, bosses, co-workers, friends, spouses, in-laws – to name a few. Getting along with and even loving others is a learned experience. We come into this world completely selfish. At the time we are born we are only required to communicate our needs.

I am not a child psychologist so I don't know exactly when this changes, but it does change when the infant learns that there are certain perimeters to his/her behavior. It is a parent's responsibility to teach their children that screaming and hitting doesn't win friends and influence people. A well adjusted child gradually learns to wait a reasonable length of time to have their needs satisfied. As a child grows and develops, it helps if they have time with other children their age. This way they begin to develop the skills for the relationships they will hopefully have all their lives. Those who become adults expecting instant gratification may not scream, but are infantile in their demands. Now, as an adult, we should have learned that we have to give as well as take.

I believe that relationships are the most important and, perhaps, the most difficult part of our lives. That's not exactly true because we often have traumas, like illness or death of loved ones that take all of our strength and faith to survive. However, basically, to be loving and giving is what really matters as we make this journey through life.

At one time in my long life, I felt that good relationships were easy. I loved everyone and assumed that they all loved me. Now I realize that was naïve. In a perfect world, we would all love one another. There would be no anger, greed, bitterness or a judgmental attitude toward our fellow man.

It isn't always easy to be loving when people in our lives are hateful. When someone lashes out at me, I usually think they have a problem and I'm usually right. I just happen to be there when they are angry and frustrated. If the anger directed at you is personal, it needs to be resolved. If it is not personal, you may be able to help a friend or family member overcome it.

My thinking has often been conflicted as regards to relationships. It is not easy. We have to learn to be flexible and not expect everyone in our lives to share our point of view. I read somewhere recently, "It is OK to be wrong. We do not always have to be right." What a concept! I can't imagine anything more healing in a relationship then to be able to say. "I was wrong and I am sorry." Why is it so hard to say this?

I have found that there are different kinds of relationships. I would like to examine them one at a time. I am not an expert, but I have learned a few things. I also have been astounded and dismayed when I have encountered hurtful behavior.

FAMILY – This should be the easiest, but is often the most difficult. So many different feelings factor into the relationships with parents and/or siblings.

We would have a family meeting about (what I thought) were important issues. I always believed that they went well – that we were able to discuss problems rationally and with good humor. It turned out that I was delusional. In talking with family members later, every participant seemed to have come away with a different viewpoint about what was being discussed.

It has always amazed me that children raised in the same family with the same parents are all so different. Each one has a different personality with different strengths and weaknesses. Their place by birth in the family seems, too, to make a difference. Often there is competition, rivalry and jealousy. Hopefully, by the time they become adults they will appreciate each others differences and become friends.

Communication is essential. Misunderstandings must be discussed and resolved to the satisfaction of both parties. Sometimes a person refuses to speak to a member of the family for real or imagined hurts. If you are the person the anger is directed toward and you do not even understand what happened, the hurt can eat you up inside. Your mind goes round and round trying to figure out what happened. Because you care so much about that family member, you have a great sadness.

There is so much that is wrong –greed, hate, intolerance. It is discouraging when we contemplate how little we, as individuals, can change all that. I decided a long time ago that if we each concentrated on making our little section of the world a more loving, caring, sharing place it would have repercussions we can't even imagine.

Sometimes we find it difficult to love a person in our own strength when we don't like their behavior. That, however, is when they need our love the most. Years ago my sister said, "Why is the most difficult child the one who needs the most love?"

The only way I know to keep your own peace of mind, is to tell yourself that the person involved is the one with the problem. In order to heal yourself, you pray for healing for that person. Surround them with your loving thoughts and pray for a resolution to the misunderstanding.

There are some people who have never learned to take responsibility for their own choices and actions. It is always the fault of someone else if they make mistakes, wrong choices or fail. It is OK to fail, but we need to learn from our failures, take responsibility for our missteps and move on. Don't take out your frustration on the people you are supposed to love.

Extended family comes to include in-laws, aunts, uncles, cousins. You are fortunate if you can immediately embrace additions to the family circle. You need to appreciate another person's strengths and tolerate their weaknesses. You need to remember that you are not perfect either.

It is possible that you will never be a close friend with acquired family members. However, you can be loving and non-judgmental. With additions to your family circle by marriages or births, try to look for the positive things they bring to your relationship. Do you immediately find fault with new people who enter your life? If you do, then you are the problem.

Some family members seem to want to stir up trouble. It is hard to deal with a person who is constantly critical of you and others. I learned long ago that you can't win an argument with them. It is best to ignore their remarks and try not to take their behavior personally. It is hard to do but possible.

FRIENDS - Some people seem to make friends so easily. Others don't have many friends. They are lonely and wish they did know how to connect with others. Let's see if we can figure out what it takes to attract others and make them want to be with us.

What are your expectations in a friendship? Sometimes we reach out to another person and there is not the response we had hoped for. Other times we seem to have an instant connection with someone and it develops into a lasting friendship. In any lasting relationship we need to be available to listen to that person's joys and sorrows. There are times when we just need someone to listen to us and love us. A true friend will be there for you when you are hurting and/or lonely.

I believe that you have to stay connected if you want to foster and maintain a friendship. Being a friend is a two way street. I do know that to have a friend, you have to be a friend. If you truly care about another person, you will plan things of mutual interest that you can do together. Are you fun to be with? Do you look at the positive things in life and not the negative? No one wants to be around a person who constantly complains and criticizes. So lighten up!

If you are lonely and want to meet new people, I would suggest joining a group with similar interests. This could be a group that does athletic activities such as hiking, climbing, swimming or it could be a book club or exercise group or meetings of people interested in crafts, etc. You might have to try several before you find one that is right for you. If you belong to a church, there are usually different activities where you can meet people and get to know them better. Also, the schools need volunteers. I have a friend who reads to an elementary group. There are countless opportunities to meet new people if you will make the effort.

CO-WORKERS – I am certainly not an expert on working relationships. Many people spend more time at the office then they do with their family and I think all of us would want it to be a pleasant place to be. Of course it needs to be a place that fosters good working conditions and reasonable expectations. Any of my knowledge of working conditions comes from my husband's office. He was a lawyer who started with a small firm which eventually grew to a very large establishment specializing in patent law. When it was small, everyone seemed to get along fine. As the firm grew, there were clashes of personalities. It seems to me that workers don't need to be best friends but they do need to treat each other with respect. Of course if someone is constantly harassing or sexually abusing you, you need to report that to a supervisor or boss. It is probably better not to get into social situations with co-workers. You could probably tell me stories – good and bad – about getting along at work.

LOVE AND LOVING

Love is present in some form in all of our relationships. What it means to each of us is such a personal emotion. What does love mean to you? Perhaps you can explain love as you have experienced it in your life. It is a word that sometimes is used loosely and with very different meanings. It can be a profound life changing experience.

Several definitions in the dictionary tell us that love is an intense affectionate concern for another person, an intense sexual desire for another person, a strong fondness or enthusiasm for something. The dictionary lists synonyms for the word love as: affection, devotion, fondness and infatuation.

There are many references to love in the Bible. My favorite is I Corinthians 13, Verses 4 & 5: Verse 4 says, "Love is very patient and kind, never jealous or envious, never boastful or proud, never haughty or selfish or rude. Love does not demand its own way. It is not irritable or touchy. It does not hold grudges and will hardly even notice when others do it wrong. It is never glad about injustice, but rejoices when truth wins out. If you love someone you will be loyal no matter what the cost. You will always believe in him, always expect the best of him. And always stand your ground in defending him. Verse 5: All the special gifts and powers from God will someday come to an end, but love goes on forever." Quotation from The Living Bible.

I believe that love is unconditional. We do not withdraw our love because someone disappoints us. No one is perfect – even us. We need to know that we are always loved in spite of our mistakes. You cannot love someone and hate them at the same time. You can love them and hate what they do.

Whenever we think of love, most of us think of the romantic attraction. However, there are so many different kinds such as love for our children, reaching out to friends and acquaintances without expecting something in return. It would be wonderful if each of us worked to make our little world a better place by loving those around us.

One problem with loving is that many people tell me that they have low self-esteem. They don't like themselves very well and often think that others don't like them. It is hard for them to accept love because they don't believe that they are worthy. This becomes a self- fulfilling prophecy as they become unlovable. Do you like yourself? That may seem like a strange question. However, if you don't like yourself you will not believe that you are worthy of the love of others.

There are many reasons for low self esteem. If children are raised in a negative environment, they will have trouble feeling good about themselves. A negative teacher can affect you for a lifetime even as a good one affects you in a positive way.

THERE IS NO PROPER WAY TO GRIEVE

It takes courage to get through a loss. Be patient with yourself.

"You can grieve endlessly for the loss of time and for the damage done therein.. For the dead and for the loss of your own lost self. But what the wisdom of the ages says is that we do well not to grieve on and on . . You can grieve your heart out and in the end you are still where you were. All your grief hasn't changed a thing. What you have lost will not be returned to you. It will always be lost. You're left with only your scars to mark the void. All you can do is choose to go on or not. But if you go on, it's knowing you carry your scars with you." Author unknown.

The above quotation speaks to me in a profound way. We cannot continue to grieve a loss indefinitely. Although there is no timetable for accepting the loss of a loved one, we need to take steps toward some resolution to our grief. It took me a long time but I finally can accept loss even though I don't understand it. Nothing I can do will bring a person back to life, but I will always remember and honor that memory.

I do know that everyone grieves differently. I have learned to never say to a person, "I know what you're going through" because the other person may be experiencing an entirely different process than what I experienced in a similar loss. So much has been written about grieving and some of it is helpful, but mostly we must find our own way.

Your life may never be the same without the ones you love. I believe that eventually it is up to each one of us to invent a new life. This might be done with a change in our job or a change in location. I do know people who want to be surrounded with memories of loved ones. Others need to move on. It doesn't mean they forget. It just means that they need to make the rest of their life worthwhile.

Some authors even identify the stages of grief. One of the most quoted is by Elizabeth Kubler-Ross from her book "Death and Dying". She lists the following stages:

Denial (this isn't happening to me!)
Anger (why is this happening to me?)
Bargaining (I promise I'll be a better person if)
Depression (I don't care anymore)
Acceptance (I'm ready for whatever comes)

Kubler-Ross continues on to explain. "Many people believe that these stages of grief are also experienced by others when they have lost a loved one." Personally, I think of these definitions as emotional behaviors rather than stages, per se. I believe we may certainly experience some of these behaviors. But, I believe just as strongly, that there is no script for grief, that we cannot expect to feel any of our emotions in a particular set pattern. I do agree that acceptance is probably the last emotion felt, and in some instances it may be the only one.

Another definition of the stages of grief is described by Dr. Roberta Temes in her book "Living With An Empty Chair – A Guide Through Grief". Dr. Temes believes that those experiencing loss express the following behaviors.

Numbness (mechanical functioning and social insulation).

Disorganization (intensely painful feelings of loss).

Reorganization (re-entry into a more "normal" social life).

These authors come to their conclusions through the observation of many people and what they tell us may be helpful. However, so much depends on the circumstances of the death of a loved one. Is this person old or young? Is the death sudden or the result of a long illness? There are as many variables as there are people. I think we need to be there for each other, but in a non-threatening way. I think we can learn from what others write even though it doesn't exactly fit our situation. It is somehow comforting to know that we are not alone in our grief.

I particularly enjoyed a book titled "My Grandfather's Blessings" by Rachael Naomi Ramen, M.D. On death and dying, she wrote "There is a growing belief that there is a right way to die, a death according to plan, where every goodbye is completed, every promise fulfilled, every conflict resolved, and everyone discovers in the end that they were loved. Occasionally things do work out this way, but life is rarely this tidy. Life is passionate and mysterious. It has its own way of working things out, and everything of great value does not come gift wrapped. There are times when death is brutal and even ugly, but all death has profound meaning. Over time each person who is genuinely touched by a death will find that meaning for themselves in their own way, even those who have been disappointed in themselves or feel they have failed someone else.

"The first meaning of all death is loss. But meaning is dynamic. Over time, new meanings may evolve that are far less universal and more our own. It is important to revisit our wounds to see what new meanings may have grown there. If we become frozen in anger and pain, it may be many years before we recognize what these are.

"Befriending life often requires accepting and experiencing loss. There is no question that great loss may have a deeper meaning and may indeed transform those touched by its terrible grace. But it is foolish to think that spiritual growth will somehow remove loss, much in the same way that an aspirin removes pain. Spiritual awakening does not change life; it changes suffering. . . .The loss is the same. Only the meaning changes. Its meaning evolves, the suffering may become less but the loss will last forever.

"The final step in the healing of suffering may be wisdom. Perhaps no suffering really heals completely until the wisdom of its experience has been found and appreciated. We do not return from the journey into pain and illness to the same house we left. We have become more and the house we will live in will be more as well, for however long we inhabit it."

I, personally, have observed many different reactions to loss. Most people believe that their experience with loss is unique. And, in many ways, it is. Each of us arrives at this place with a different accumulation of experiences.

Do we have a support system of family, friends and a religious belief? We need to know that people are there for us. I have found that some people like to be alone to work through their grief. Others want to be surrounded with their loved ones. I can't help but say, "Whatever works." There's a quote I like and I don't know the author. It says, "If God brought me to this; He will see me through this.",

People also grieve other losses besides the death of a loved one. Some of these would be the following:

Loss of a job

Loss of a relationship - either a lover or a friend

Loss of health caused by a life-threatening illness or a chronic health problem.

Loss of money – especially from a bad investment.

Some parents grieve when their children grow up and leave home.

Life changes all the time and we need to meet changes as challenges. When I am presented with a crisis, I say, "What am I supposed to learn from this experience?" Hopefully, it will be that I become more compassionate and empathetic when others are suffering.

In the book "Dearly Beloved " by Anne Morrow Lindbergh she writes about a couples loss of a son. "He (the husband) had learned then about the isolation of grief, even for those in the same grief. Grief can't be shared. Everyone carries it alone, his own burden, his own way."

When I speak abut grieving, I speak from personal experiences. I need to give you a short background about my personal grieving, It was during the depression in the 1930s. My Father had survived a series illness before I was born, but it left him with numerous disabilities. My Mother had taken a position organizing the PTA and speaking to groups all over the State. She was able to do this because her Mother lived with us. My Mother was on a speaking tour across the State when she was killed in an auto accident. She was only 43 years old and needed by so many people. I was 13 and my sister was 15.

I think now about how devastating it must have been for my Father because he was so dependent on her. My sister and I were thrust into big responsibilities at a very young age and I regret that I thought mostly about me and not my Father.

There were no counselors or help with grieving in those day. If there had been, we wouldn't have been able to afford that help. Instead, it was like a curtain was drawn over my Mother's life. No one talked about her. We were just supposed to go on some way without her. Because of my age, I remember being mostly angry that she had left us.

I was going to church at the time but that didn't seem to help much. Actually, it was many years before I found my faith. It was a retired minister friend who helped me accept her death many years later. I finally accepted it but I will never understand the reason why.

Several years after my Mother was killed so tragically, my Grandmother had a paralyzing stroke. She couldn't walk or talk. We tried to manage for awhile, but eventually my Father asked her other children to take care of her. Gram had two sons who lived in Minneapolis and a daughter on a farm in South Dakota. The daughter came and took her back on the train to the farm. I still remember saying goodbye. She was crying because she didn't want to leave us. She didn't live long after she left. She had always been part of my life and I never saw her again.

My Father died when I was 26 years old. The Second World War had just ended. I had married Ben just before Pearl Harbor and we had gone to Washington, D.C, so he could go to Law School there. He was in the Navy five years, two years on Guadacanal in the South Pacific. When he returned, he was stationed in Seattle and we had our first child. At that time we were moving back to Washington, D.C. so Ben could finish Law School. My sister and I had urged our Father to take the train to visit relatives in Minneapolis.

Ben and I and our three month old baby had recently arrived in D.C. when I received a long distance phone call that my Father had fallen downstairs at my Uncle's home in Minneapolis and was in a coma. I flew there the next morning with my baby and my Father died the following morning. He never regained consciousness and I have always hoped that he could hear me in the little time we had together. Baby and I had to take him home, arrange services and take care of legal matters. It was a month before I could return to D.C.

As I write this, it brings the pain back and it sounds as if my life has been filled with grieving. However, these deaths occurred over a period of many years. There were many times in between when I knew happiness and fulfillment. I don't believe that I had great expectations but I was always hopeful that life would get better. I do believe that I have appreciated the good times more because of the events of my life. And it certainly has made me more understanding of others.

HOW IS YOUR ATTITUDE?

I would like to begin this chapter with a quote from Charles Swindohl titled "Attitude". "The longer I live, the more I realize the impact of attitude on life. Attitude, to me, is more important than the past, than education, than money, than circumstances, than failure, than successes, than what other people think or say or do. It is more important than appearance, giftedness, or skill. It will make or break a company…a church…a home. The remarkable thing is we have a choice every day regarding the attitude we will embrace for that day. We cannot change our past… we cannot change the fact that people will act in a certain way. The only thing we can do is play on the one string we have, and that is our attitude…I am convinced that life is 10% what happens to me and 90% how I react to it. And so it is with you…we are in charge of our Attitude."

It is easy for people to say to us, "Stay positive. Don't be negative." But how do we accomplish this? If we live a long life, there are going to be many ups and downs. No one in this journey through life should expect to avoid dealing with sadness and loss. It is how we deal with these conditions that shape our personality and our relationship to the other people in our lives. I believe each of us would choose to be a blessing in the lives of those around us.

I work diligently to remain positive and cheerful. I certainly am not always happy but I'm good at pretending. It is so easy to slip into habits of anxiety, criticism and self-pity. We need to stop this kind of thinking by reciting our gratitude for all the good things in our life. Develop a habit of thanking others for their help and kindness by writing notes, emails or phone calls.

One of the gifts my Mother gave to me when I was young was teaching me how to write thank you notes. We didn't receive much at Christmas but there was a much anticipated box from my Aunt Stella who lived on a farm in South Dakota. It was filled with homemade gifts and my Aunt told me years later that she stayed up nights to make them because she didn't have money to buy gifts. There was nothing in the box of monetary value, but it was so much fun to get a box in the mail. Mother told us to write thank you notes within a week or the gifts would be returned.

AND WE BELIEVED HER. It started a lifelong habit of expressing gratitude. I passed it on to my children and they have passed it on to their children. You will be amazed at how that lifts your spirits and even your health. The benefit to you and the recipient of your gratitude cannot be measured.

If we are fortunate enough to live a long life, we should be very grateful for our longevity. Our ability to do everything we used to do has diminished but I try to be grateful for what I have left. It is so easy to complain about changes and inconveniences. Following are some things you might be grateful for every day.

If you have your physical health, be grateful.

If you have your mental health, be extremely grateful.

If you can still live on your own, be grateful.

If you have loving family members and friends, be grateful.

We need to have a sense of humor and not take life too seriously. One example of what strikes me as funny, was a picture of an old couple kissing each other in the local paper on Valentine's Day. It said each of them was 100 years old. I thought "Isn't that sweet." Then I read the accompanying article and it said that they were married when they were 87 years old. Somehow, featuring them on a holiday about love struck me as very funny because when I looked at the picture of them I was thinking of the long, loving life they had spent together.

Many old people do not have a sense of humor, but perhaps they never have been able to see the humorous side of life. They are depressed because they can't do everything they used to do when they were younger. To me, that is sad and useless.

I would like to recommend a humorous book that I have enjoyed. It is Tales of the Truly Unpleasant by Steve Johnston. Steve worked for the Seattle Times for many years and wrote a weekly column called Sunday Punch. This book is a collection of these columns and when I feel sad I read them and they make me laugh. Johnston had serious health problems but he still saw the humorous side of everyday events. He wasn't trying to change the world. To me, his writings help me see the humor in our everyday lives.

I have written elsewhere to explain how religion (or faith) helped me to navigate all the pitfalls of this journey. I am not suggesting that my way is your way. I am just hopeful that some of the things I have learned will assist you.

WHAT MAKES YOU HAPPY?

Most of us spend a lifetime chasing this elusive condition. There seems to be a lot of "what ifs" and "if only" in our lives as we pursue something that remains beyond our grasp. Often we don't even know what we are chasing but think we will recognize it when it appears in our lives.

I do know that lasting happiness is not about money and possessions. We spend so much of our lives acquiring "things" and so-called "keeping up with our neighbors". Of course it is good to have an adequate income. The question is how much is enough? I grew up during the great depression and then the Second World War. My sister once said to me that everyone that came home from the Second World War, worked hard at finishing school and/or starting a job. Most were married and many had children and their big ambition was to buy a home in the suburbs with a swimming pool. They finally made it, went outside, looked around and said, "Is this it?"

Having gone through the process of downsizing and moving to a smaller place, I do know that we have many possessions that we don't need. I have written about that process in another chapter. I have said that we spend 75% of our lives collecting things and the next 25% trying to give most of it away. I have really enjoyed giving possessions away to family and living with less.

I know contemporaries who are downsizing and moving into retirement communities. That is a good positive decision. Months after they have moved, however, some of them tell me that they still have boxes to unpack. I say if they still have not completely unpacked some possessions, they don't need them and should give them away. What you don't need could be a wonderful help to someone else and there are organizations in almost every community that will pick up household items and furniture and distribute them to others.

Looking back over my long life, I don't believe that happiness is a condition that a person can sustain. I have known periods of great joy and times of anxiety and sadness. There is a wonderful happiness that I can identify with loving and being loved. Then there is a happiness that I call peace and contentment and I have to work to achieve that. I don't think we can ever be happy if we are always worrying about ourselves and others. I have learned to be accepting and grateful for the love and caring that I receive from friends and family.

In his book "Ageless Body, Timeless Mind" Deepak Chopra says "the emotion of love releases powerful chemicals in our body.........We need to love others unconditionally and nonjudgmentally". I get so much positive feedback from family and friends. When we feel we're loved, it gives our body a warm glow. We need to express our love to others ------tell them, write them, but somehow communicate. Our family and friends can't read our minds. If we are loving, we get so much in return.

As we attempt to understand ourselves or others, it helps to read what our "experts" believe is the path to happiness. I highly recommend "Fire In The Soul" by Joan Borysenko, PhD. The author addresses many of the questions we all ask; such as, why do human beings suffer? Is there a personal God who punishes us? She takes us on a journey as she searches for a meaning to life. Borysenko tells us that she looked for answers in the study of philosophy, religion and psychology, but feels she learned the most from her own trials and those of friends, family and clients. In other words, we learn by living. If we can get past our anger, fear and depression, each crisis presents us with an opportunity for growth.

Certainly all of us want to lead happier, healthier lives and that is possible if we can release the past and move forward. How can we do that? This book discusses the problems of worry, anxiety and the inability to forgive ourselves and others and keeps us from enjoying our life. Worry has no constructive purpose and is different from planning which is goal oriented.

All of us need help in our journey through life. In my opinion, we also need to read books that nourish our souls, that teach us how to cope, to heal relationships, to forgive, to love ourselves and others and to live with joy in spite of circumstances.

SPIRITUAL JOURNEY

Searching For Meaning

I began writing this book with the purpose of providing information on planning ahead as we are aging. Since then, I have decided that it might be valuable for you to know how I arrived at this old age. Perhaps my experiences might be helpful to you.

My life hasn't always been easy. I have had devastating tragedies and life-threatening illnesses. I believe that I have survived because of a resilience of spirit and an optimism that if today is bad, tomorrow will be better. I do seem to always have had the belief that whatever the crisis, I would be helped through it. Maintaining a positive attitude is so important and we need to work on that. If I start to think negative thoughts, I do stop and count my blessings.

One of the most important things I learned in my spiritual development has been learning to release the past so that I can live fully in the now. I know that I bring my past with me to any new beginning, but I try to take only whatever adds to my enrichment or growth. I carry with me the understanding I have gained from my experiences, but I try to let go of excess baggage of guilt and regret.

My search for spiritual understanding has certainly been an important part of my life. I am not suggesting that my way should be your way. It just might help to explain my journey.

My journey toward faith was a long one. I read many books on religion and philosophy and I had many questions that I felt no one ever answered to my satisfaction. It reminds me of the story of Thomas in John 20. Jesus had appeared to the disciples after the crucifixion when Thomas was not present. When the other disciples said they had seen the Lord, Thomas replied, "Unless I see the nail marks in his hands and put my finger where the nails were, and put my hand into his side, I will not believe it." John 20:25.

According to John, Jesus appeared again to the disciples when Thomas was present and said to him, "Put your fingers here, see my hands. Reach out your hand and put it into my hand. Stop doubting and believe." Then Thomas said, "My Lord and my God" to which Jesus replied, "Because you have seen me

you have believed: blessed are those who have not seen and yet have believed." John 20: 26-29.

Then in Mark 11:24 Jesus says, "Therefore I tell you that whatever you ask for in prayer, believe that you have received it and it will be yours." The sweet mystery of life has come down through the ages. It is the answer to every need and the source of every blessing. Maybe the answer is that it is so simple, we overlook it. There were times when I looked for some complex answer or tried on my own to make things right. When I stopped striving and searching outside myself and simply said, "God I want you in my life," everything changed.

During the time of my spiritual quest, I spent a great deal of time with a wonderful retired minister and we discussed many aspects of religion. The day finally came that I realized that I did not need the answers to all of my philosophical questions. I only needed trust. On that day I was freely given faith by the grace of God. It was certainly not anything I had earned. It has been an awesome presence in my life ever since.

At a time of great crisis in my life, I spent a day in prayer. On that day God said to me, "I am here. I have always been here." And I realized that He never deserts us, we desert Him. This presence is always available to us, but we need to ask for it. I remember that on that day I finally surrendered my ego to God.

I had experienced numerous crisis situations in my life and was proud of the fact that "I" was always able to cope. There was a lot of "I" did this and "I" did that in my life. In this life-threatening situation, I finally said, "I cannot do this anymore by myself and I turn my life over to you, God."

The following day was amazing. I felt as if a light was flooding around me all day and I had an inner peace that I had never known before. All the fear of my present situation was completely gone. Since that time, I have come to believe that each of us is an instrument of God and, if we will let Him, He works through us to accomplish good. None of us ever uses all of our potential and talents, but if we will listen to that Higher Power it will direct us to accomplish things we never thought possible. We need to ask for direction and then we need to listen. This applies not only to our health but to all aspects of our life. We are all so busy that we don't have any quiet time and we certainly are not going to be given direction unless we clear our minds of all other distractions. I truly believe that God will work through us in every aspect of our life if we will let Him. He will rejoice with us in our blessings and grieve with us in our sorrows.

The following quote is attributed to St Francis de Sales. "Do not look forward to what may happen tomorrow: the same everlasting Father who cares for you today will take care of you tomorrow and everyday. He will shield you from suffering or He will give you unfailing strength to bear it."

I didn't grow up in a spiritual family. I can't remember ever talking about faith. My Father went to a Congregational Church that was a block away from our house. I can't remember my Mother ever going to church. My Grandmother lived with us and she liked to read Unitarian material although I don't remember her attending church.

Our next door neighbors attended the Christian Science Church and my sister, Ruth, and I started going to church with them. I'm not sure how old we were when we started, but my attendance continued on into adulthood. Christian Scientists have a daily reading from the Bible followed by quotations from the Science and Health written by Mary Baker Eddy. At church, there is no minister. They have what is called a lay leader who reads the lessons that the members had been reading all week. Everything seemed low key – no choir, no fund raisers, no wedding ceremonies, no funerals and no church related activities that I recall. I must have received something intellectually because I continued to go there for many years.

There were many things that were right about this religion. I think I have carried the philosophy of that experience throughout the rest of my life. Reading something inspirational every morning is an excellent way to start your day and I still do that.

Their philosophy of positive thinking has always sustained me. Their founder, Mary Baker Eddy, wrote the "Science and Health with Keys to the Scripture". It is a beautiful piece of literature and I feel that it must have been inspired by God.

I believe that I moved on from the Christian Science church because I was looking for something more. I'm not sure but I probably quit going when my Mother died. That was a very bleak period. Here we were, my sister and I, two young girls and no one helped us with this tragedy. Looking back, I realize that I was very frightened and very angry. I couldn't believe in a God that would let my Mother die in a car accident. My Mother was so vibrant and accomplishing so much good for the community. It goes without saying that our family needed her desperately. I have never understood why she had to die at such a young age, but I have learned to accept it.

It was years later that the retired minister, Lou Dunnington, helped me confront those issues. He said he didn't believe God makes these things happen and that He grieves with us. That belief was very comforting to me.

I met Dr. Dunnington after we moved to Mercer Island. There was an article in the local paper that he was going to start a new church on property owned by the Methodist Church. I learned later that he was a retired Methodist minister who had led a large church in the Midwest. He and his wife moved to Mercer Island to be near their son and family. He soon became bored with his inactivity and called Methodist headquarters for something to do. They told him that they owned property on Mercer Island and asked him to start a church. He was a marvelous preacher and the congregation grew quickly.

I attended the church regularly but I was not a member. I remember Dr. Dunnington pressuring me to join and I kept saying that I wasn't ready. Finally, one day he said, "Why don't you stop thinking about what the church can do for you and think about what you could do for the church." I joined and have been an active member ever since.

Eventually, heart problems forced Dr. Dunnington to retire but he still filled in as guest preacher in other churches. He and I had a wonderful close relationship and we spent many hours together.

I know people who tell me that they have always had a deep religious faith. I envy them. I think perhaps my religious struggle was shaped by the devastating events in my early life.

Our churches are filled with people who are searching for something to fill the void in their lives. Dr. Dunnington used to say, "I wish I could tell you that if you come to church a light bulb will come on."

He certainly started me on the road to believing and said, "Keep working at it; it takes a lifetime."

There were many earlier years when I didn't go to church at all. Then I visited a variety of churches waiting for that light bulb to go on. I have explained the life-changing experience I had the second time I was diagnosed with cancer in a book I wrote titled "Cancer Saved My Life". To think that all I had to do was say sincerely, "I can't do this anymore by myself and I surrender my ego to you, God." What a relief to know that I was surrounded with God's grace and love. I realized that I always had been, but I just didn't know it.

I used to pray asking or begging for things or healing, I would pray saying "Thy will be done, God, but this is the outcome I would like." Now I start my prayers with, "God, I turn these concerns over to You and I promise not to take them back." Since I do believe that God does heal, I simply thank Him in advance for the healing I know is coming. I do not know how or what form that healing will manifest itself, but I do know that it will be for my good or for those who are in my prayers.

I do not believe that there is any recipe for spiritual enlightenment. Individuals can share their faith, but each person must find their own way. I don't have the words to describe the inner peace I was given when

I finally welcomed God into my life. I do wish all of you the blessings I have received.

DRIVING MISS DAISY

A very serious decision for senior citizens is when to quit driving. I think it is the hardest decision we make because it takes away so much of our independence. No one told me that I needed to quit driving and I had an excellent driving record. I made this decision several years ago because I felt that my skills were diminishing. Now I have to plan ahead and depend on others to drive me. I am amazed and amused at others my age and the excuses they make to stay on the road. They are so often in a state of denial about their abilities. We need to admit to ourselves that we have reached old age. And that is not so bad considering the alternative. As we age, we do lose more and more, but we need to be grateful for what we have left.

Why did I quit driving? Even though I had a very good driving record it seemed prudent to take myself off the road. I had to admit to myself that my eyesight was failing, my depth perception was off and my reflex reactions had certainly diminished. The problem seems to be that so many elderly people refuse to admit that their driving ability has lessened. The son of a friend of mine said, "It's better to quit driving five minutes before you have a catastrophe, then five minutes after." That is so true. This is a problem as we live longer and longer.

Do you remember the movie "Driving Miss Daisy"? I do and I always envy that she had a marvelous chauffer to take her wherever she wanted to go. Now that would be a wonderful solution for each of us. However, a full time driver is costly and out of the reach of most of us. So we need another solution. Since I quit driving, I have found that I need to plan ahead for assistance doing those everyday errands. I keep a list everyday of items needed.

I believe that the State Licensing Department has a responsibility when it comes to licensing older people to drive. Perhaps there should be a cutoff age as to when a license will be issued. Certainly there should be an age when a drivers test is required. I had a good friend who was driving until he was 100 years old. He picked me up once in his 90s to meet friends for dinner. It was a frightening trip. He constantly drifted over the center line and missed our turnoff. I never accepted a ride with him again but I'm sure he would have told you that he was a good driver.

A friend sent me a very funny email about an elderly lady and her driving. At least it struck me as humorous and an example of an older person in denial regarding the real problem. It had funny pictures of an old lady at the wheel of her car and the email quoted her as follows:

"I bought a bumper sticker that said, HONK IF YOU LOVE JESUS. You wouldn't believe how many people love Jesus - everyone was honking at me." The email went on in this vein and the lady never admitted that she might be the problem. The story goes on in the same humorous vein as she tells about being the front car at a stop light and she was the only one who manages to get through before it turns red again. She says, "I hated to leave all those cars behind because they were all honking at me."

Now, how do we deal with our transportation needs. Most of us have family or friends who will help out. And believe it or not, if you figure all the costs of owning a car, you can even afford to take a taxi at times. I have a lady who works for me once a week for a few hours. She cleans, does my grocery shopping, and helps me with errands when needed.

In my community, there is a listing called Family Services. If you tell them your needs, they will assist you in a resolution or direct you to the proper agency for help. Many elders move to retirement communities and many of these provide transportation.

There is a listing of retirement homes and costs in the back of this book that should help in living decisions. The list doesn't include every retirement and nursing home in the area. However, it should give you a good idea of questions to ask about costs and services.

There are agencies that list themselves as being expert at helping you or a family member find an Adult Home. Apparently, many of them receive a fee from the owners of the Adult Home for referring a possible resident. So if you do need help, I would suggest calling a State agency to check them out. Different states probably have different regulations. Try to make sensible decisions so you will be in a place you can afford and where you will be reasonably happy.

It is a wonderful privilege to live a long time and we need to be grateful for the added years. It is a great blessing if we are financially secure and reasonably healthy. So instead of complaining about what we have lost in the process of aging, let us be thankful for what we have left. Many days I don't feel just super. I often have vague aches and pains but I'm still maintaining with a little help.

I cannot say often enough to stay flexible about necessary changes in our living situation. Try to be loving to everyone, especially to those who are tryng to help us. Reach out to others who are struggling with life situations by phone calls, emals and notes.

I remember the good times and am thankful that I survived through the sad and/or difficult times in my life.

THOUGHTS TO PONDER

Don't be part of the problem – Be part of the solution. If you are not part of the solution, learn to pray about it and then let it go.

I give all my concerns to God – Let Go Let God and I promise not to take them back.

Love and compassion. Love doesn't judge. Compassion is forgiving. We may be disappointed in the behavior of someone we love, but that doesn't mean we withdraw our love. We may say, I'm disappointed in your choices, but I still love you.

Those who have been given much must give back – not only money but time and talent.

Gratitude. Make it a practice to start each day being grateful for all of our blessings. No matter how bleak or sad our life may seem, there is always something to be grateful for. What are your gratitudes?

As we age, we lose more of our ability to get around and that's hard, but we need to be grateful for what we have left.

Money may buy happiness but it cannot hold it.

I don't always have to be right. It's OK to be wrong sometimes. I believe there are no more healing words then, "I was wrong and I'm sorry."

I would rather pray and discover there is no God then not pray and discover there is.

If God brings you to it, He will help you through it.

This is the day the Lord has made – rejoice and be glad in it.

Let there be joy in my life – worthwhile projects – gratitude –good relationships.

Help me to be patient and understanding.

Help me to live my life with calmness – no anxiety – each day a blessing. Happiness is a choice. Trust God. I am not dependent on others to make me happy.

Follow God's direction in my life.

Be accepting of relationships as they are. Know that each person in my life is doing the best they can. Know that I can change me – not them.

Gratitude for all my blessings – home, health, financial security, family and friends.

Thank you, God, for the good that is available to me right here and for the good that is on its way to me.

So much gratitude, God, for my loving family.

Archbishop Desmond Tutu: "Being courageous does not mean never being scared. It means acting as you must even though you are undeniably afraid."

Lena Horne: " It's not the load that breaks you down, it's the way you carry it."

Thank you Lord. Thank You for taking care of me today. Thank You for what you are going to do for me tomorrow. For whatever comes into my life I thank You.

READING LIST

Inspirational books by authors who believe we can lead healthy, happy lives. All of these books emphasize the mind/body connection.

DISCIPLINES OF THE SPIRIT by Howard Thurman. In this book the author writes about commitment, growing in wisdom and stature, suffering, prayer and reconciliation. Thurman examines in depth the questions we all ask about life. He delves deeply into the human experience in a search for meaning to our existence. I have had the privilege of meeting Howard Thurman and hearing him speak. His presence reinforced his deep spiritual commitment for me.

FIRE IN THE SOUL, A New Psychology of Spiritual Optimism by Joan Borysenko, PhD. Dr. Borysenko is a cell biologist, a licensed psychologist, an instructor in yoga and meditation, and one of the architects of a discipline called psychoneuroimmunology. This is a long word but simply put it is the connection of the mind/body in wellness. The author addresses many of the questions we all ask, such as, why do human beings suffer and is there a personal God who punishes us? She takes us on a journey as she searches for the meaning of life. Borysenko tells us that she looked for answers in the study of philosophy but feels she learned the most from her own trials and those of friends, family. and clients. In other words, she learned by living. The author says, "Some of the healthiest people I know are those who have had to heal from the most challenging situations and, in the process, have gained insight and wisdom far beyond what a 'comfortable' life would ordinarily provoke."

LOVE, MEDICINE AND MIRACLES by Bernie Siegal, M.D. This book was a runaway best seller when it was published in 1986 and it was one of the early books to explore the connection between the body and the mind. It is the story of the author's own growth from an overworked surgeon with no joy in his chosen profession to a medical practitioner grateful for the dramatic changes in his life and those of his patients. The book is full of concrete suggestions for a better, healthier life, some of which are good nutrition, exercise, having fun, loving yourself and others, relaxation and meditation.

FORGIVE AND FORGET by Lewis B. Smedes. Perhaps the most difficult thing to attain in our lives is the ability to forgive ourselves for past mistakes and to forgive others who have hurt us. We need to examine our thoughts and feelings carefully to see if the inability to forgive is restricting our ability to live life with love. Read this book. It will have a profound effect on how you view yourself and others.

A PRETTY GOOD PERSON: WHAT IT TAKES TO LIVE WITH COURAGE, GRATITUDE, INTEGRITY OR WHEN PRETTY GOOD IS AS GOOD AS YOU CAN BE by Lewis B. Smedes. The author has a special knack of going to the heart of problems that get in the way of our ability to live our lives with joy and love. In this book he discusses gratitude, courage, integrity; taking charge, grace and love. Lewis Smedes believes we need to feel good about ourselves. We need to feel that we are doing the very best job we can in this journey through life.

PEACE, LOVE AND HEALING by Bernie Siegal, M.D. There is such a wealth of material in this book. Those of you who are familiar with Dr. Siegal's writing, lectures and seminars know that he is not only talking about physical healing, but healing of relationships, attitudes, priorities, and goals in life. How we think does affect our immune system even though the medical community is slow to accept the fact. This book provides techniques to attain the best quality of life possible.

AGELESS BODY, TIMELESS MIND by Deepak Chopra M.D. Our society has conditioned us to believe that we are inevitable victims of sickness, aging and death. The author believes it is possible to reverse these assumptions. Chopra says, "We are the only creatures on earth who can change our biology by what we think and feel." The author believes that joy and fulfillment keep us healthy and extend life. It is important to continually set new goals and take on additional challenges. Central to the entire theme of the book is the message that we need to love and be loved. There are all kinds of love encompassing the romantic, parent for child, child for parent, for friends, for humanity and, perhaps, the most important of all, the unselfish love that expects nothing in return.

This is a very partial list of helpful books. There are so many that will assist you in learning how to live well each day. They all emphasis the benefits of positive thinking.

COST AND SERVICES OF RETIREMENT HOMES

The following section gives you a sampling of the retirement communities in this area. It may be slightly different where you live, but it gives you an idea of costs and services and what questions to ask. You need to evaluate several things before making a move to a retirement community. The information included here was provided by the retirement homes in the year 2011.

    A. Finances. What you can afford.

    B. Location

    C. Services. Assisted Living and Nursing Care.

The biggest problem in planning for your old age is how much money you will have. As you will see, retirement communities are expensive and may not be possible for you. Some cities have low cost retirement communities. In my area, these area apartments are called SHAG. They provide living quarters at a very reduced price and their advertisements feature comfortable looking apartments.

There is a wealth of information available on the computer. If you go to GOOGLE and type in Senior Services, you will receive a wealth of information about wellness, nutrition, senior center activities, day health centers and other services.

If you don't have access to a computer, look up Senior Services in the phone book. Keep calling and asking questions until you find the help you need. Another excellent resource is AARP and they will be happy to send you information on a wide range of subjects relating to aging. Hopefully, you have family to assist you.

I cannot emphasis enough how important it is for each of us to plan ahead before we are older and in poor health. You can work at downsizing your possessions long before you plan to move. Most of us have much more "stuff" then we need or will ever use.

Name --- Aljoya (Parent Company ERA)
Address --- 2430 76th Avenue SE
City --- Mercer Island
ZIP --- 98040
Phone --- 206-230-0150
Buy in Fee --- Yes From 399,000 to 1,125,000. Based on size of apt.
Amount --- See above
Refundable --- 90% (Discuss this with management)
1 Bedroom --- Yes
Size --- Beginning at 800 square feet
Monthly Fee --- $3,000. Additional Fee for second person
2 Bedroom --- Yes
Size --- Up to 2,000 squre feet
Monthly Fee --- $3.280. Additional Fee for second person
Washer & Dryer --- Yes
Number of Meals --- 25 a month
Cleaning --- Yes, Once a week
Services --- A range of assisted living with additional costs
Assisted living ---Includes assistance with personal hygiene
Nursing Care --- No
Cost --- N/A
Medicaid --- No
Transportation --- Available

Name--- Bayview Retirement Community

Address ---11 West Alhoa Street

City --- Seattle

Zip --- 98119

Phone --- 206-284-7330

Buy in Fee --- Yes

Amount --- $50,000 to $431,000 $17,500 addition for second person

Refundable --- Negotiate at time of entrance

1 Bedroom --- Yes

Size --- 645 square feet

Monthly Fee --- $2,495 to $2,980

2 Bedroom ---Yes

Size --- 975 square feet

Monthly Fee --- $3,350 to $4,165

Studio and Alcove Apts. --- 324 to 486 square feet

Washers & Dryer --- Linen and towel service

Number of Meals --- Lunch and dinner each day

Cleaning --- Weekly light housekeeping

Services ---Use of Wellness Center. Emergency call response

Assisted Living ---Yes

Cost --- Home care services are billed in half hour increments

Nursing Care --- Yes

Cost --- Depends on level of care

Medicaid --- Ask Management

Transportation ---Available

Utilities --- Yes

Outside Help ---Ask Management if resident can hire outside help

Name --- The Bellettini

Address --- 1115 10th Avenue NE

City --- Bellevue

Zip --- 98004

Phone --- 425-450-0800

Buy in Fee --- Yes

Amount --- One Time Residency Fee $3,000

Refundable ---No

1 Bedroom --- Yes

Size --- 700 to 2,400 square feet

Monthly Fee --- $3,500 to $5,200

2 Bedroom --- Yes

Size --- See Above

Monthly Fee --- Starting at $4,900

Washers & Dryer --- Yes

Number of Meals --- $400 food and beverage credit (per person)

Cleaning --- Weekly

Services --- Includes 2 hours per month of complimentary concierge service

Assisted Living --- Yes

Cost --- Ask Management

Nursing Care --- No

Cost --- N/A

Medicaid --- Ask Management

Transportation --- Complimentary transportation service

Utilities --- Yes (except private telephone and Internet access)

Outside Help --- Ask Management if you can hire outside help if needed.

Comments --- Add $600 for double occupancy

Name --- Covenant Shores

Address --- 9150 Fortuna Drive

City --- Mercer Island

Zip --- 98040

Phone --- 206-268-3000

Buy in Fee ---Yes

Amount --- $86,500 - 532,500

Refundable --- Yes. Amount depends on length of stay and services

1 Bedroom --- Yes

Size --- 633 to 920 square feet, Deluxe 1,085 to 1,100 square feet

Monthly Fee --- $1,849 to $2,126

2 Bedroom --- Yes

Size --- 909 to 1,182 square feet, Custom 1,300 to 1,852 square feet

Monthly Fee --- $2,159 to $3,659

Studio --- Yes

Size --- 466 to 526 square feet

Monthly Fee --- $1,515

Washers & Dryer--- Free use of Washer and Dryers

Number of Meals --- Three per day

Cleaning --- Weekly Housekeeping

Services --- Paid Utilities (except telephone and internet)

Assisted Living --- Yes

Cost --- Varies depending on services needed

Nursing Care --- Yes

Cost --- Daily Rate $295 - 389

Medicaid --- Ask Management

Transportation --- Available

Utilities --- Yes

Outside Help ---Ask if this possible if you are not able to live alone.

Comments --- Add $878 for second occupant of apartment. Covenant Shores provides all levels of care. Costs vary

Name --- Emerald Heights Retirement Home
Address --- 10901 176th Circle NE
City --- Redmond
Zip --- 98052
Phone --- 425-556-8220
Buy in Fee --- Yes
Amount --- Varies according to the plan
Refundable ---Varies from 50% to 100%
1 Bedroom --- Yes
Size --- 701 to 904 square feet
Monthly Fee --- $1,850 to $2,906
2 Bedroom --- Yes
Size --- 904 to 1,630 square feet
Monthly Fee --- $2,906 to $4,164
Studio/Cottage --- Yes
Size --- 900 to 1,276 square feet, Numerous floor
    plans to choose from
Washers & Dryer --- Yes
Number of Meals --- One meal per day
Cleaning --- Weekly Housekeeping
Services --- Yes
Assisted Living --- Assisted Living if needed or skilled
    nursing care
Cost ---Included in monthly payment
Nursing Care --- Yes
Cost --- Included in monthly payment
Medicaid --- Yes
Transportation --- Scheduled transportation service
Utilities --- All utilities except telephone
Outside Help --- Ask Management

Name --- Exeter House
Address --- 720 Seneca Street
City --- Seattle
Zip --- 98101
Phone --- 206-622-1920
Buy in Fee ---One time Community Fee
Amount --- $1,000
Refundable --- No
1 Bedroom --- Yes
Size ---615 to 860 square feet
Monthly Fee --- $3,300 - $4,000
2 Bedroom --- Yes
Size --- 980 to 1100 square feet
Monthly Fee --- $4,500-$5,300
Studio/Alcove --- Yes
Size --- 370 to 490 square feet
Fee --- $1,900 to $2,800
Washers & Dryer --- Personal Laundry $15 per load
Number of Meals --- Ask about how many per month
    included
Cleaning --- Weekly
Services --- Parking $120 per month
Assisted Living --- Some help available in daily living
Cost --- Depends on assistance
Nursing Care --- No
Cost --- N/A
Medicaid --- No
Transportation --- Available
Utilities --- Included
Outside Help --- Ask Management

Name ---Horizon House

Address --- 900 University Street

City --- Seattle

Zip --- 98101

Phone --- 206-382-3100

Buy in Fee --- Yes

Amount --- $29,800 to $500,000 Entrance Fee of
$10,000 for 2nd person

Refundable --- Yes (50% to 90%)

1 Bedroom --- Yes

Size --- 500 to 780 square feet

Monthly Fee ---$1,646 to $$1,701

2 Bedroom --- Yes

Size --- 800 to 1430 square feet

Monthly Fee --- $2,169 to $2,666

Washers & Dryer --- Yes

Number of Meals --- Optional $150 credit included
in monthly fee

Cleaning --- $33.25 per month

Services --- Yes

Assisted Living --- Yes

Cost --- Depends on level of care needed

Nursing Care --- Available

Cost --- Each patient evaluated individually

Medicaid --- Available if a patient is eligible

Transportation --- Available

Utilities --- Yes

Outside Help --- Ask management if you can hire
outside help to stay with you

Second Person --- Monthly Fee is $871

Name --- Ida Culver House Broadview
Address --- 12505 Greenwood Avenue North
City --- Seattle
Zip --- 98133
Phone --- 206-361-1989
Buy in Fee --- No
Amount --- N/A
Refundable --- N/A
One bedroom --- Yes
Size --- 517 to 1,350 square feet
Monthly Fee --- $2,520 to $4,395
2 Bedroom --- Yes
Size --- See Above
Monthly Fee --- $4,530
Washers & Dryer --- Yes
Number of Meals --- 2 Meals per day
Cleaning --- Weekly
Services --- Yes
Assisted Living --- Yes
Cost --- Depends on services required
Nursing Care --- Yes
Cost --- Varies depending on services required
Medicaid --- Ask Management
Transportation --- Available
Utilities --- Yes
Outside Help --- Ask Management if you can hire
    outside help if needed
Comments --- Cottages Available at $6,280 add $775
    for second person

Name --- Island House (Owner Merrill Gardens)
Address --- 7810 SE 30th Street
City --- Mercer Island
Zip --- 98040
Phone --- 206-236-0502
Buy in Fee --- No
Amount --- One Time Fee of One Month's Rent
1 Bedroom --- Yes
Size --- 622 square feet
Monthly Fee --- From $2,950 Second Occupant $600
Pet Fee --- $800
2 Bedroom --- Yes
Size --- 875 square feet
Monthly Fee --- $3,850 Second Occupant $600
Studio --- Yes
Size --- 430 square feet
Fee --- From $2,200
Washers & Dryer --- Yes
Number of Meals --- Two meals per day
Cleaning --- Yes
Services --- Yes
Assisted Living --- Extra charges for help with
    medicine, bathing, etc.
Cost --- $300 to $2000
Nursing Care --- No
Cost --- N/A
Medicaid --- Yes
Transportation --- Available
Utilities --- Included in rent
Outside Help --- Ask management if you can hire
    outside help if needed

Name --- Mirabella
Address --- 115 Fairview Avenue North
City --- Seattle
Zip --- 98109
Phone --- 1-877-447-5658
Buy in Fee --- Yes
Amount --- $279,000 to 699,000
Refundable --- 90%
1 Bedroom --- Yes
Size --- Not Listed
Monthly Fee --- $2,893 to $3,241
2 Bedroom --- Yes
Size --- 1,607 square feet plus 90 foot deck
Monthly Fee --- $3,300 to $3,473
Washers & Dryer --- Yes
Number of Meals --- Basic plan - 30 meals per month
Cleaning --- Housekeeping every other week
Services --- Yes From basic care to total care in
    nursing facility
Assisted Living --- Yes
Cost --- A certain amount of care included in
    monthly fee
Nursing Care --- Yes
Cost --- Depends on level of care
Medicaid --- Ask management
Transportation --- Complimentary to local
    appointments
Utilities --- Yes
Outside Help --- Every level of care a resident needs is
    provided

Name --- Pacific Regent of Bellevue
Address --- 919 109th Avenue NE
City --- Bellevue
Zip --- 98004
Phone --- 425-646-9808
Buy in Fee --- Yes
Amount --- $139,000 to $447,000
Refundable --- Depends on what plan you have chosen
1 Bedroom --- Yes and 1 Bedroom plus Den
Size --- 700 to 1,015 square feet
Monthly Fee --- $2,033 to $2,131
2 Bedroom --- Yes
Size --- 960 square feet
Monthly Fee --- $2,621 to $2,890
Washers & Dryer --- Yes
Number of Meals --- Choice of lunch or dinner
Cleaning --- Weekly
Services --- A Variety of Wellness Services
Assisted Living --- Includes tray meals, assistance in personal care
Cost --- Depends on services needed
Nursing Care --- Nursing Facility if needed
Cost --- Included in monthly fee
Medicaid --- Ask management
Transportation --- Van and private transportation available
Utilities --- Included in monthly Fee
Outside Help --- Ask management if you can hire outside help if needed